Why Restorative Justice?
Repairing the Harm Caused by Crime

Why Restorative Justice?
Repairing the Harm Caused by Crime

Roger Graef

edited and additional material by
Marian Liebmann

CALOUSTE GULBENKIAN FOUNDATION, LONDON

Dedication

To Martin Wright, whose vision of restorative justice has not obscured his commitment to rigorous scholarship. This vision inspired me to see the potential of restorative justice to change our lives.

Published by the
Calouste Gulbenkian Foundation
United Kingdom Branch
98 Portland Place
London W1B 1ET
Tel: 020 7636 5313

ISBN 0 903319 92 6

British Library Cataloguing-in-Publication Data
A catalogue record for this book is available from the British Library

Designed by Andrew Shoolbred
Printed by Expression Printers Ltd, IP23 8HH

Distributed by Turnaround Publisher Services Ltd,
Unit 3, Olympia Trading Estate, Coburg Road, Wood Green, London N22 6TZ
Tel: 020 8829 3000, Fax: 020 8881 5088,
E-mail: orders@turnaround-uk.com

Cover photo: Still from *In Search of Law and Order – UK* (Channel 4).

Contents

Author's Acknowledgements

John Harding, one of the pioneers of restorative justice in Britain, has been extremely helpful. Turi Munthe came to me wanting television experience and found himself deeply immersed in restorative justice, helping to assemble the book. Felicity Luard and Ben Whitaker of the Gulbenkian Foundation gave me this stimulating commission, and my publishers Richard Johnson and Andy Fishwick at HarperCollins allowed me to interrupt my work on a longer critique of the justice system which has this concept as its conclusion. Guy Masters helpfully read the manuscript for errors. Marian Liebmann selflessly and generously fleshed out the text with essential references and useful information while editing the book extremely skilfully. I am most grateful for her substantial contribution. The dedication to Martin Wright, author of many seminal books in this area, only hints at his support in guiding me through the shoals of this sensitive area.

The author and publishers would like to acknowledge the following organisations for providing case studies: Boughton Hall Youth Justice Service, Chester; Crime Concern Mediation and Reparation Service, South West Hampshire; Kent Intensive Supervision and Support Programme; Leeds Victim-Offender Unit; Maidstone Mediation Scheme; Mediation UK; Sheffield Victim/Offender Mediation Project; and Texas Victims Services.

Foreword

Most criminal justice systems focus exclusively on the processing and punishing of offenders; achieving any improvement for the future of either victims or offenders unfortunately has little or no priority. Our present legal machinery often makes both victims and the local community feel they are sidelined if not irrelevant, and offenders are rarely made to confront the results of their crimes. Restorative justice aims to redress this balance, and at the same time achieve a more constructive longer-term outcome for the future of all concerned. It is one of the most hopeful and encouraging initiatives in the otherwise gloomy field of law and order.

Family Group Conferencing has been successfully used since 1989 in New Zealand (the country which also helped to lead the world on votes for women and on ombudsmen). As Roger Graef describes in Chapter 3, its central feature is to bring young offenders and their victims together at structured meetings, alongside other people affected by the crime, and any witnesses and neighbours who may be relevant to a particular offence – in much the same way as the tribal setting for the justice dispensed by our ancestors. At the end, suitable reparation is agreed, whether a sincere apology and/or financial compensation or work in kind.

The UK Branch of the Gulbenkian Foundation was enthusiastic about helping to fund two pilot projects in restorative justice in 1998. Under the recent Crime and Disorder Act, a range of new approaches is being tried in the UK to improve the youth justice system. At present it is estimated that only three per cent of young offenders are sentenced by courts, usually after long delays and too often unsuccessfully. The charity Bristol Mediation, which specialises in 'new approaches to conflict resolution', was asked to coordinate with the local police and social services a new multi-agency project in Bristol, Victims and Offenders in Conferences (VOICES).

The other project helped by the Gulbenkian Foundation is, encouragingly, being pioneered and energetically developed by Thames Valley Police, the Chief Constable, Charles Pollard, Chief Superintendent Caroline Nicholl (now in the USA) and Chief Superintendent Ralph Perry. The principles of restorative justice are being extended not only to discipline cases, but also to local schools to deal with bullying, vandalism, racism and other anti-social behaviour. From 1998 the Thames Valley Police has been employing the concept in virtually every suitable case when it cautions an offender.

The indications are that restorative justice is cost-effective, but the most important effect it achieves is a long overdue wider public access to, together with involvement in, our system of justice. Such ideas deserve wider consideration and therefore I am very pleased that Roger Graef, whose skilled documentaries on policy and youth justice have evoked wide praise, has written this book.

Ben Whitaker
Director, UK Branch of the Gulbenkian Foundation, 1988–99.

Introduction

Restorative justice is an idea whose time has come – again and again. It has ancient roots and has been the bedrock of tribal justice for several millennia. Yet we have been largely unable to grasp its meaning within the context of rising crime, the search for law and order, and the crisis in criminal justice. Nor have we understood its potential for handling conflict in other institutions.

Until very recently, the task of our criminal justice system has been mainly to judge events in the past, leading to the conviction and punishment of offenders. I have become convinced that this is an unsatisfactory way to deal with the needs of individuals and the community in coping with the damaging experience of crime. Nor does it help to reduce the chances of its happening again. Whatever the outcome, too many victims feel cheated, and too many offenders fail to take responsibility for their actions.

There is now the opportunity for change in the UK. After two decades of experiment in pockets around Britain, from June 2000 new legislation (the Crime and Disorder Act 1998) expects Youth Offending Teams across England and Wales to arrange for young offenders to repair the harm they have caused to victims. It is not before time, and should begin a sea change in our understanding of such encounters.

The philosophy of restorative justice is to work with people in their communities in the aftermath of crime. The restorative approach recognises that crime can have profound effects on individuals, on their families and communities, on the offenders themselves and on their families. It seeks to redress the harm done to each of these parties, and directly to empower each to make decisions about reparation and future behaviour rather than having such decisions imposed by courts or professionals.

Informal resolution is the most widespread form of restorative justice. It is not an exotic, obscure concept: it happens constantly in families when a parent or third party mediates between warring family members. It happens in schools, at work, between friends, or couples splitting up or trying to stay together – making up, or at least making good the damage done. Often the local bobby, known to his community and who knows them, quietly mediates between disputants rather than bringing them to court.

Mediation often involves explanations on both sides, for the issue or misunderstanding to be cleared up. Along the way, revelations may cause tears and rage, embarrassment and shame. It may take several sessions before issues are resolved to parties' joint satisfaction. But when and if they are, the feeling of having achieved something, having moved through the problems or dispute, reaching forgiveness, acceptance or compromise, is tangible. Something has happened. Something has ended. We can move on.

Mediation

There are many kinds of mediation which provide a restorative approach in institutions and in the community. The process and details of each mediation are kept confidential, although the outcome or agreement is usually in the public domain, especially if there is a legal issue.

- Peer mediation in schools
- Family mediation for child issues in divorce
- Family group conferences concerning child welfare
- Neighbour mediation
- Multi-party mediation
- Community conferences
- Medical mediation
- Employment and workplace mediation
- Commercial mediation
- Environmental mediation
- Political or international mediation
- Victim/offender mediation

This restorative approach is recognised in the recent reforms in civil justice (1999), which emphasise the use of alternative dispute resolution (ADR) and mediation before cases are taken to court, and provide legal aid for mediation in the same way as for court cases.[1]

Restorative justice is not just about face-to-face mediation. It spans other kinds of making good: from reparation and community service to indirect mediation via a go-between, to community sentencing boards, and community mediation of local conflicts. In a growing number of schools, it can be seen in anti-bullying programmes based on peer mediation. It is being used by social services in the form of Family Group Conferences to make positive plans for children at risk of going into care.

Victim/offender mediation is appropriate when there is an identified victim (though practitioners of conferencing would say there is always a victim) and an offender who acknowledges guilt. It is concerned with mediation of criminal justice matters, and their wider causes and impact. However, it is important to acknowledge from the start that the use of restorative justice in the criminal justice field is limited to those offenders who admit their responsibility; and both offenders and victims must be willing to take part. But this is not such a hindrance, as the vast majority of cases result in guilty pleas.

Restorative justice means just what it says: restoring the balance of a situation disturbed by crime or conflict, and making good the harm caused to the individuals concerned. The word justice implies a concern for fairness in the process, and a recognition that any outcome must be seen to be just by both parties. The positive nature of restorative justice also places great emphasis on future behaviour.

Research points to strongly favourable views of the experience among those who take part in it, when compared to their experience of the conventional justice system.

- Victims are given the chance to express themselves and be involved directly in ways that have not traditionally happened in courts.
- Offenders also approve of it, which may appear at first sight more surprising; it is no 'soft option' for them, for contrary to popular belief, they usually find it much more challenging to face their victims than to be part of the impersonal court process.

1 The new Civil Procedure Rules came into force on 26 April 1999, discussed in H. Genn, *Mediation in Action: Resolving court disputes without trial* (London, Calouste Gulbenkian Foundation, 1999).

Hard evidence about success in prevention of offending is by its nature difficult to amass, and requires thorough and long-term research. However, research studies are ongoing and there are many encouraging pointers (described in Chapters 4 and 5).

This short book cannot be a complete account of restorative justice. I have attempted to set down the main principles and practices, and to demonstrate their value and effectiveness with accounts of cases from different parts of the world, including the UK – from Northern Ontario to Northampton, from Texas to Thames Valley – many of which I have witnessed or filmed. If the views of users matter, then restorative justice deserves to be taken seriously, and I am convinced that it deserves a central place in our criminal justice procedures.

Chapter 1

The Need for Change

This chapter considers the need for change in our traditional justice system, by looking at the experiences of victims and offenders, and at court practice.

For some victims crime is little more than a nuisance. But for others – individuals and families – it is too often a painful, dispiriting experience. The rise of the national charity Victim Support (see page 23) has brought practical help and comfort to many victims in the last 20 years, but the resources available do not meet all their needs.

The court process

It comes as a surprise to many victims that they appear in court only if they are needed as witnesses, not in their own right. There they are sometimes subjected to gruelling cross-examination, which feels to them like 're-victimisation' – living through the crime all over again. They are allowed to speak only about legally defined 'facts' – not about what the crime meant to them.

Although court cases are conducted in the name of the victim and the community, they seem to operate mostly according to the requirements of the courts. The result is that many victims feel marginalised, and distant from 'their' process. Sometimes the sentence itself becomes the focus of a sense of outrage and unfairness. There is little sense of closure, forgiveness, or encouragement for victims to get on with their lives by putting the damage caused by the crime behind them.

For some victims, having 'their' offender convicted and punished may actually increase the risk to them. In serious cases, family and friends of the accused may terrorise victims waiting to appear as witnesses. Hence the reluctance of so many witnesses and victims to report crimes, make statements or testify in court.

Even when victims are awarded compensation, the impact of suffering on those who may depend on them is often left out of the calculation. Moreover victims with a criminal record receive reduced or no compensation from the Criminal Injuries Compensation Authority. Once convicted of a crime, it would seem that a person's right to be considered a victim is greatly diminished. And yet the line between victim and offender is seldom so clear.

For offenders, the court process does the opposite of what is intended. It can help to distance them from what happened. Although the spotlight is on the person in the dock, the offender takes little part in the proceedings. Watching passively as their lives are discussed in complicated language by strangers, offenders often cannot hear or understand what is going on. It is their lawyer's job to argue on their behalf and get them off, whether they are guilty or innocent. Sometimes their lawyer may even blame the victim for bringing 'the crime' on themselves, as in many rape cases.

The threat of serious punishment makes the legal system mindful of protecting the rights of the accused. But this often defeats the goal of accountability. So some guilty people plead not guilty in the hope of escaping punishment. Others plead guilty to reduce their sentence, rather than out of remorse and a desire to make good the harm they have done. When they do this as a tactic, it is not only the state that loses, but the victim and the community.

The offender, if found guilty, is given a sentence, but in some cases their families are also punished. For example, mothers are imprisoned even for relatively minor offences, despite the impact on their children. Wage earners who support whole families have their livelihoods put at risk even by short sentences, imposed to 'teach them a lesson' rather than to protect the community. The longer-term damage to the offender's family is ignored.

The courts are often accused of unfairness by both victim and offender. The convicted person and their supporters may see the sentence as unjustly heavy, while the victim and their friends see it as too soft. The local media may chime in with their disapproval. This leaves magistrates or judges in a 'no-win' situation where the sentences they pass are criticised on all sides.

This dissatisfaction is compounded if, as often happens, the trial comes months after the original offence. The long period of waiting prevents healing and closure for the victim, and focuses the offender's thoughts on the outcome of the court case rather than on putting right the harm done. The offender may even have forgotten the crime or that it had consequences for someone else. Speeding up the process, as the Home Secretary is attempting to do, is laudable but does not resolve the basic problem. Indeed, Martin Wright (former Director of the Howard League for Penal Reform, Policy Officer of Victim Support, and founder member of Mediation UK) argues that in many cases it does not give the victim enough time to consider whether to take part in restorative processes.

The most damaging effect of the court process is that it prevents parties from communicating at a human level. The victim cannot tell the offender the effects of the crime, or ask questions that have been haunting them since the crime itself. The offender cannot answer such questions or express remorse even if they feel it – which many do once they have met their victim through mediation.

A chance for change

The renewed interest in restorative justice in Europe and North America is born of the growing recognition that reliance on punishment alone has failed to deliver the sense of fairness, satisfaction and security we hope for from the justice system.

Restorative justice operates within the framework of the law and is overseen by the courts to ensure that the outcome is reasonable. It can in some cases be the only intervention, diverting offenders from court, usually for less serious crimes. For more serious offences, restorative justice may form part of the response.

Restorative justice offers a different paradigm. It looks forward, offering the chance to translate a negative experience into a more positive framework. By restoring substantial control of 'their' conflict to victims and offenders themselves – as well as friends and families in some situations – it encourages all parties to become involved in establishing a basis from which to progress.[2]

2 Howard Zehr has compared the effects of the retributive and restorative justice systems. See page 63.

But, as Susan Herman, Director of the National Victims Center in Washington, has pointed out, mediation cannot be the answer to all victims' needs. Most crimes are not reported, and of those that are, most are not solved. Offenders may not wish to take part in mediation. And those that do may have such limited resources that victims' long-term medical, psychological or financial needs are unlikely to be met. Some seriously damaged victims will still need long-term support that can only come from the state. Nevertheless, very real benefits are reported by victims and offenders who have taken part in mediation.

Jason's story

Jason, a persistent young burglar, had been in court many times from the age of 15. Whatever the magistrate said went in one ear and out of the other. For him, the risk of punishment was an occupational hazard – it was certainly no deterrent. As a child, Jason had often been left on his own with only a box of cornflakes to eat while his mother went to the pub. His first thefts were of food from local shops. He then joined other young-sters on the estate to become an active burglar.

Jason often returned to the scene of the crime again and again. He had stolen from the house of a woman nearby more than 11 times, taking cash, cameras and television sets – which she replaced each time. He also stole goods of sentimental value, whose loss added to her distress.

Such burglaries are often justified by young offenders like Jason on the grounds that things stolen will be replaced – and upgraded fraudu-lently, they assume – through insurance. That view implicates the victims in gaining from their own loss, a kind of rough compensation. Jason saw such cheating as all part of the game. Until they have been burgled them-selves, young offenders often feel no empathy for the victims of the harm they have done, for the deeply unsettling experience of being invaded by strangers, nor for the pain of losing apparently worthless personal items.

Jason's most frequent victim found her successful life as a single mother, running a business from home, deeply affected by him. His burg-laries terrified her into transforming her pleasant open-plan home into a fortress, adding more alarms and barriers each time. Jason saw these not as a deterrent but as a challenge. She finally installed iron gates which he told me were useless: he could break in from the back.

Although Jason had been caught often – and spent time inside – no one had told him about his primary victim. Despite having touched each others' lives, the two had never met. I told Jason what he had done to her life. He seemed genuinely embarrassed, and expressed real regret. He liked the goods he had stolen, and the buzz of defeating her anti-burglar devices, but did not want to make her unhappy. I found myself astonished – not by his remorse, but by his surprise that he had damaged another person's life. Despite all the punishments, Jason never connected his actions with the effect on his victims.

As it happened, there was no mediation scheme in his area at that time, so when Jason was caught and convicted, he simply went to prison again, leaving his victim temporarily relieved, but already anxious at what would happen when he came out once more.

Were he given the chance to meet his primary victim, and to undertake to avoid her house in future, Jason could help rebuild her confidence, sense of safety and well-being. He could also provide vital information – subject to confidentiality – about the vulnerability of other victims, which would have helped Crime Prevention Officers to improve local safety.

Chapter 2

Principles of Restorative Justice

Restorative justice is based on several principles which differ from those of our traditional criminal justice system.

- The victim is given the opportunity to have a more central role in the judicial process.
- The primary goal of the restorative justice system is not punishment but making good the harm done by offending – for the victim, the community and the offender.
- Offenders take responsibility for their actions as a precondition to addressing the harm that they have caused.
- Offenders become aware that crime is committed, not against an abstraction, but against someone real – a person like themselves – and also against their community, who are affected by what has happened.
- Crime and conflict are seen as affecting relationships between individuals, rather than between individuals and the state.
- The process aspires to be as inclusive as possible, not exclusive. It involves individuals who are left outside the court system altogether by conventional justice.
- Proceedings and agreements are voluntary for all parties. People are offered the chance to take part in mediation, or to make or accept reparation, but it is up to them to accept it or not.
- The process is always confidential, but the outcome and agreements can be made public.

Putting the victim rather than the state at the centre of the judicial process is a paradigm shift of real significance. No longer is proving guilt or innocence the main concern in order to impose or escape punishment. Instead, the primary issues are:

What harm was caused?
What was its wider emotional context and impact?
Why was the harm done?
What will it take to put things right?
What will prevent it happening again?

Restorative justice works to heal the damage to individuals caused by conflict and crime. In many situations, this damage occurs to both victims and offenders, and often also affects those who are involved with or depend on them – who are ignored by conventional legal processes. This can be a wide circle of family, friends and employees.

These principles of restorative justice lead to some important guidelines for practice:

- Direct communication between victim and offender must always be voluntary. Offenders can be encouraged to take part, to see the impact of their actions. If their own victims do not want to participate, offenders may be able to meet other victims whose offenders were not caught or who declined mediation.
- Those working with victims and offenders should co-operate to ensure the programme operates in a neutral way, balancing concern for victims with concern for the offenders.
- Mediation can help the sense of healing and closure for everyone involved. But abusive offenders can re-victimise the victims. Hence the need for proper preparation with both parties over time. This is especially true when the victim is vulnerable, and the crime is serious.
- Mediation must never be a substitute for the court process for accused people who say they are innocent. It must not be prejudicial to the offender.

The Human Rights Act

There has been some discussion of how restorative justice fits in with the implementation (from October 2000) of the Human Rights Act 1998, which enables the British courts to apply directly the provisions of the European Convention on Human Rights. Article 6 of the Act emphasises the importance of a fair trial and due process in any court proceedings, and includes the concept of 'proportionality', i.e. the use of the least restrictive sentence, which must also have a stated constructive purpose. International principles and practice advocate courts being used as a last resort for juveniles, and diverting young people at an earlier stage. So there could be a problem with the Youth Justice and Criminal Evidence Act 1999, which covers England and Wales (see page 56), because it attempts to use restorative justice in a court process, rather than diverting young people from court. The fact that it is a court process also raises issues about legal representation and the role of the victim – are they observers or participants? – which have yet to be resolved.

Giving victims and offenders such a central role at the sentencing stage worries those on the bench who feel under increasing pressure to ensure consistency of sentencing across the country. However, the same sentence can have very different impacts on different offenders and victims. Restorative justice is no more 'inconsistent' than traditional justice. It operates within the law; courts can oversee the limits of the reparation or compensation agreed and prevent excesses in any direction.

The aims of restorative justice are to put things right for the victim and to help offenders take responsibility for what they have done; therefore it should actually provide a *more* satisfactory outcome for many victims and offenders than they might have experienced otherwise. It is worth noting that other members of the Council of Europe, like Germany and Austria, have had the European Convention as part of their legal systems for decades. They have implemented more far-reaching restorative justice measures than the UK. The spread of victim/offender mediation in Europe is also part of a world-wide momentum towards restorative processes.[3]

3 K. Akester, *Restoring Youth Justice* (London, Justice, 2000) and conversations and correspondence with Kate Akester, Justice; Jim Dignan, University of Sheffield; Rob Mackay, University of Dundee; Guy Masters, Goldsmiths College, University of London; Martin Wright, July 2000.

Charlie's story

Charlie was 17 and was already on a court Supervision Order when he burgled a building and stole equipment to sell. He had been in care since the age of four, but at 16 had to move to a bedsit on his own. Although he had some support, he had no family or friends, and quickly turned to drugs to mask his pain and loneliness. He needed money for the drugs, and sold the equipment for £50.

When he got caught, Charlie discovered that the building he had burgled was a day centre for disabled people, and the equipment he'd stolen had been bought with donations and through fund-raising events. For the Centre, the burglary was disastrous. Charlie felt really awful and that he was just a bad person. His Youth Offending Team (YOT) worker suggested mediation and referred the case to the local mediation service.

After interviewing Charlie, the mediators contacted the manager at the Centre. The disabled people who used the Centre had not been able to go there for weeks after the burglary, as replacement equipment was hard to obtain. They could not understand what had happened and were very upset. The Centre also had to spend a lot of extra money making the place more secure, and the staff worried whether they would be broken into again. Everyone was very angry with the perpetrator and wondered what sort of person would do this to a charity.

A meeting was arranged between Charlie and the Centre manager. Each side told their story. The Centre manager said that Charlie's circumstances did not excuse what he had done. Charlie agreed and said, 'I can only say, I did not know about the disabled people and I am really, really sorry.' He offered to do some work at the Centre if it would help make amends.

The manager accepted Charlie's apology but declined his offer of help, as staff would not feel safe with him there. What she did want was an assurance that Charlie would go on a drug rehabilitation programme and sort himself out. The mediators were able to say that the YOT worker was helping Charlie to do this, and also find him suitable job training.

The Centre manager promised to convey Charlie's apology to all the staff, who would feel reassured, knowing that Charlie was genuinely sorry for what he had done. She said she felt the session had been really worthwhile. The mediators pointed out that Charlie had not apologised because of any gain in terms of a lesser sentence, but because he wanted to do his best to make things right.

Chapter 3

A Brief History

Restorative justice is not a new idea. In England it formed the basis of Anglo-Saxon law before the Normans arrived. It was part of many earlier legal traditions, including Roman law. It was inserted in the earliest known written laws, the Code of Hammurabi of c.2000 BC.[4] Most traditional systems of justice in Africa and Asia were based on restorative justice. Aboriginal and Native American justice is based on restoration and reparation. In these societies, justice between people is inextricably linked to the religious and everyday framework of the people whose lives it affects. The philosophy of restorative justice embraces a wide range of human attributes: healing, compassion, forgiveness and mercy – as well as mediation and reconciliation, and sanctions when appropriate.

After the Norman Conquest, William the Conqueror turned the justice system in England away from the restorative model. He defined crime as disruption of 'the king's peace' and fined offenders in the King's Courts, in part to benefit the king's pocket. English monarchs increasingly took the revenue from reparative justice in their kingdoms, for financial and political reasons. Their control of the judiciary reinforced their power by linking local justice back to the crown. Kings justified their intervention on the grounds that the wrong done to an individual extended beyond his family because it affected the community. This model of justice asserts that crime harms the state, and that the state should react by punishing the offender. Thus today legal procedures invariably begin with some version of 'Rex/Regina v' or 'The People vs'.[5]

---

4 D. van Ness, ed., *Restorative Justice: Theory and practice* (Washington DC, Justice Fellowship, 1989).
5 For an in-depth discussion of the history of justice in relation to mediation and restoration, see M. Wright, *Justice for Victims and Offenders*, 2nd edn (Winchester, Waterside Press, 1996), pp. 22–32.

The rise of victim support and mediation services in the UK

In the second half of this century, British Probation services made many valuable innovations in the field of juvenile justice, but concentrated on rehabilitating the offender. One of the first steps towards focusing on the needs of victims was the Criminal Justice Act of 1972, which established Compensation Orders (money to be paid by offenders) where crime had resulted in 'injury, loss or damage'. Initially these Orders were in addition to other punishment, but from 1982 Compensation Orders could be the sole penalty for an offender. A further Act in 1988 required the courts to consider a Compensation Order in *every* case of death, injury, loss or damage. If they did not, they had to give reasons.

In practice, Compensation Orders are linked to offenders' ability to pay, so many victims cannot be fully recompensed. And many offenders see it as an extension of the fine, because it is collected by the same office. Crucially, they do not connect it with the victim.

Community Service Orders, established in 1972, were also seen as a restorative measure, though not directly benefiting the victim. Offenders make reparation by working on projects which benefit the local community.

The first Victim Support scheme in Britain was started in Bristol in 1974, when the Bristol Association for the Care and Resettlement of Offenders thought of getting offenders to meet their victims so that they could fully appreciate the effects of their actions. The founders of the scheme realised they knew nothing about victims of crime, and set out to research their needs. Victim Support is now a well-known national charity and all areas of the country now have a local service, with many courts also offering a witness support service.

The first recorded victim/offender mediation and reparation service was started in Canada in 1974 by Mennonites in Kitchener, Ontario. A probation officer, Mark Yantzi, took two young men to apologise and make amends to 22 victims whose houses they had vandalised.[6] This idea was taken up elsewhere in North America

6 H. Zehr, *Changing Lenses: A new focus for criminal justice* (Scottsdale, PA, and Waterloo, Ontario, Herald Press, 1990) pp. 158–60.

and then in the UK. The first victim/offender mediation project in the UK was established by South Yorkshire Probation Service in 1983, and many other local initiatives followed.

Victim Support helped supporters of mediation and reparation to form an association in 1984 – FIRM (Forum for Initiatives in Reparation and Mediation), later relaunched as Mediation UK. Some ministers like Douglas Hurd and David Mellor became interested and the Home Office agreed to fund pilot reparation programmes in Cumbria, Leeds, Wolverhampton and Coventry from 1985–7.

The last three programmes, all organised by probation services (working with adult offenders), were so successful that they continued with local probation service funding. Home Office research showed that these initial services were biased towards offenders, so the services changed their practice to become more victim-oriented. Although some mediation services were just for young offenders, most catered for all ages of offenders and victims.

However, in the early 1990s political attitudes hardened under Michael Howard's 'prison works' ethos at the Home Office. Mediation lost its political momentum. Although mediation services are now offered in many parts of Britain, they still do not cover the whole country.

Restorative justice in New Zealand

One of the first formal legal changes to incorporate restorative justice into law came in New Zealand in 1989. New Zealand and Canada have taken different routes to restorative justice from the US and Britain, rediscovering ancient practices and using them in their criminal justice systems. After some experimentation, the New Zealand government passed the Children, Young Persons and their Families Act, which introduced an intermediate stage between arrest and sentence for serious cases for a Family Group Conference to take place. This is a procedure based on the principles of restorative justice. It was developed from ideas for helping families with a young person in danger of going into care, and then extended to deal with juvenile offending.

In Family Group Conferences, juvenile offenders and their extended families are invited to attend, as are victims and their supporters. The professionals who take part include a police youth aid officer, the offender's teacher or social worker, and (where applicable) a youth advocate. Guided by a facilitator, the group explores the factors that led to the offence, and the effects that it had on the victims. Concentrating on repairing the damage and preventing further offending, the Conference seeks to produce a plan that will see appropriate measures taken to make good the harm and assist the young offender. An important part of the process is that the offender and their family are given time in private to come up with a plan that is then discussed by the whole Conference.

Eighty per cent of less serious cases are diverted from court to informal measures, often restorative in nature. Of the remaining twenty per cent, Family Group Conferences are used instead of the court process, or in more serious cases, to develop the recommendations made to the court in the pre-sentence report. If the judge accepts the plan it will normally form the basis for a three-month court order. If all conditions of the plan are completed, the case is discharged. Justice is deemed to have been done.

The use of Family Group Conferences is now expanding in many other countries. Although based on Maori culture, with its tightly knit community, it has also worked well with white families and offenders in New Zealand. A variation of this conferencing was developed in Australia and both forms are now being practised in the US, the UK, and in other countries.

Restorative justice in the UK and Europe

Recent legislation for England and Wales is providing a new opportunity for restorative justice. The Crime and Disorder Act 1998 provides for Reparation Orders to be carried out by young offenders to benefit their victims, or if victims do not want to be involved, to benefit the community. Although victim/offender mediation is not specified – it must be voluntary to be meaningful – it is seen as the appropriate way to arrange direct reparation.

In the last decade there has been a general surge of interest in restorative justice throughout Europe. Several countries now have restorative legislation. Others are introducing victim/offender mediation alongside their criminal justice system, as has been the case in the UK until now. In October 1999, in Leuven, Belgium, some 24 countries attended the newly formed European Forum for Restorative Justice conference.

Does it work?

Research into and evaluation of the success of restorative justice initiatives has taken many forms. Generally victims show great satisfaction with the process, as do offenders – even when they are merely offered it but decline to take part. A reduction in crime is harder to prove, but there are optimistic pointers. Some findings are included in the next two chapters.

Chapter 4

The Victim

The impact of crimes – even attempted ones – on vulnerable victims can be enormous. Their security is shattered. Moreover, they often blame themselves for what happened. They also suffer a stigma from being victims, as friends and neighbours often feel awkward and unsure what to say, and stay away.

The growth of Victim Support has been of inestimable help to many victims. Victim Support volunteers visit and provide short-term emotional and practical help to victims of burglary, violence and other serious crimes. They provide a listening ear when others are too upset to do so. And they can help with practical problems such as locks, insurance, filling in forms and other needs arising in the aftermath of a crime.

However, Victim Support cannot answer victims' questions about the offender. Courts are concerned only with punishment, and sometimes compensation. Yet research by Mark Umbreit and Annie Roberts of the University of Minnesota has shown that these personal issues are more important to victims than punishment. Of victims taking part in mediation, 73% wanted an apology, 80% said they wanted answers, and 90% wanted to tell the offender about the impact of the crime. The number of victims who wanted restitution was much lower: 65%. Most victims said their main reason for taking part in mediation was their desire to stop their offender reoffending.[7] Of course not all victims want to take part in mediation. They may decline the offer because they are too fearful or too busy, or because the offence was minor.

7 M. Umbreit and A. Roberts, *Mediation of Criminal Conflict in England: An assessment of services in Coventry and Leeds* (St Paul, MN, University of Minnesota, Center for Restorative Justice and Mediation, 1996), pp. 19–23, cited in M. Wright, *Justice for Victims and Offenders*, 2nd edn (Winchester, Waterside Press, 1996), pp. 38–9.

Nevertheless they generally appreciate the offer and in the vast majority of cases feel it is appropriate.[8]

Victim Statements provided to the bench before sentencing seemed a step in the right direction. These were designed to provide victims with a voice in the court system. They were piloted in six areas in the UK in 1996–7. But the research showed very mixed results, as the statements seemed little different from victims' original statements to the police. Victims rarely knew what use the courts made of them, if any, and often felt confused and let down. Courts were wary of passing sentences which depended solely on the effect the crime had on the victim.[9]

While politicians still talk about 'getting tough' on offenders, it is important to note that many hundreds of victims have expressed their willingness to meet their offenders and talk to them. Punishment is not their goal, safety is. Despite the political rhetoric about vicitms, their willingness to try restorative approaches is driven by the lack of help and attention received by victims from the criminal justice system. They see mediation as giving them a way of rebuilding confidence and control over their lives.

The 1998 British Crime Survey showed a surprisingly high level of interest from victims in a restorative or reparative meeting with their offender. Forty-one per cent said they would accept such an offer, fifty-six per cent said they would not, and three per cent were unsure. Fifty-eight per cent were interested in reparation.[10] However, these figures concern only a hypothetical interest in restorative justice. Victims who have actually been through the process are even more positive (see page 30).

Mediation addresses victims' need for:

- reassurance that the offence will not happen to them again
- an explanation as to why they were chosen – many victims

---

8 Crime Concern, *Evaluation of the VOICES Project* (Woking, Crime Concern, 1999).

9 C. Hoyle, E. Cape, R. Morgan and A. Sanders, *Evaluation of the 'One Stop Shop' and Victim Statement Pilot Projects* (Bristol, University of Bristol, Department of Law and London, Home Office Research, Development and Statistics Directorate, 1998) and R. Morgan and A. Sanders, *The Uses of Victim Statements* (Bristol, University of Bristol, Department of Law and London, Home Office Research, Development and Statistics Directorate, 1999).

10 J. Mattinson and C. Mirrlees-Black, 'Attitudes to crime and criminal justice: Findings from the 1998 British Crime Survey'. Research Findings No. 111 (London, Home Office Research, Development and Statistics Directorate, 2000).

are haunted by the sense that they are in some way to blame
- putting a face to the crime, and asking questions of the offender
- an opportunity to explain how the crime has affected them
- an apology and some form of reparation, if appropriate.[11]

These needs are finally gaining official recognition in Britain. In a major step forward for a service hitherto focused on offenders, the Association of Chief Officers of Probation in 1996 urged that, as a matter of principle, victims of crime should be able to communicate with the offender (subject to the offender's consent and proper safeguards). Under the Victim's Charter, the Probation Service now has a much greater responsibility towards victims in its work with those who have suffered serious crimes.

This is progress, as within the probation culture there has been reluctance to become involved with victims. This may be because historically their role has been to work with offenders; but I also believe that some probation officers find it hard to relate to and support offenders if they are too aware of the damage they have done. Perhaps this is because the more human and vulnerable offenders appear, the harder it is to imagine them capable of cruelty and violence.

When probation services do become involved in mediation, they face criticism from some victims' groups for focusing too much on the offender. Probation workers may see restorative justice as merely another accessory in the toolkit of offender rehabilitation. But where they have learnt the lesson about being victim-centred, local probation services run some excellent mediation services.

Moreover, clashes of interest are rare in practice. Marshall and Merry stress that, while mediation can help both parties, victims' interests should take priority.[12] They summarise mediation as helping parties 'to a constructive, revealing and influential experience that relieves the pain of victimisation on one side, while it assists self-realisation and behavioural reform on the other.' In other words, both sides should gain from it.

11 Mediation UK, *Victim Offender Mediation Guidelines for Starting a Service* (Bristol, Mediation UK, 1993), p. 1.
12 T. Marshall and S. Merry, *Crime and Accountability* (London, HMSO, 1990).

Assessing the value of mediation to victims

Assessing the value of mediation to victims is important. The measurement of reoffending is a very inexact science, but fear of crime – and the way victims feel about being attacked again – can be measured before and after mediation. The results of research to date are encouraging. Umbreit studied four victim/offender mediation programmes involving juveniles. Before mediation, 25% of victims feared re-victimisation; after it, only 10% did.[13]

In another study with Coates, Umbreit recorded that 79% of victims involved in mediation in Albuquerque (New Mexico), Austin (Texas), Minneapolis (Minnesota) and Oakland (California) expressed satisfaction with the way their cases were handled, compared to 57% not involved in mediation. These results show that victims benefit considerably from mediation.[14]

German research into victims shows that most want a greater chance to participate in criminal proceedings. Only a minority preferred to be merely witnesses. Half expressed willingness to meet their offender to negotiate a settlement.[15]

Research studies in the UK show similarly high rates of victim satisfaction. In 1994 research by West Midlands Probation Service showed that half the victims where an adult offender was involved, and four out of five where a juvenile offender was involved, accepted mediation. Eric Morrell, former Chief Probation Officer of West Midlands, said their experience was 'invariably positive'.[16]

In the Leeds Victim-Offender Unit in 1996–7, 58.3% of victims said they were very satisfied with the service, 33.3% fairly satisfied and 8.3% satisfied – there was no dissatisfaction. Slightly lower percentages were satisfied with the outcomes. In the MARVEL mediation scheme for young offenders in North Wales in 1997, 89% of victims said they would recommend the service to a friend. In the Aberdeen service in 1996–7, this figure was 92%.[17]

---

13 M. Umbreit, *Victim Meets Offender: The impact of restorative justice and mediation* (Monsey, NY, Criminal Justice Press, 1994).

14 M. Umbreit and R. Coates, 'Cross-site analysis of victim-offender mediation in four states' in *Crime and Delinquency*, 39 (4), October 1993.

15 Klaus Sessar, 'Restitution or punishment: An empirical study on attitudes of the public and the justice system in Hamburg' in *Eurocriminology*, 8–9, 1995, pp. 199–214.

16 Eric Morrell, 'Victim-Offender Mediation' in *Victim-Offender Mediation Conference, 9 February 1994, Collected Papers* (London, ISTD and Bristol, Mediation UK, 1994), p. 7.

Claire

Claire, a 38 year old single mother, and her eight year old son Max were victims of an aggravated burglary. The burglar, Sean, broke into their house at night and terrorised them. Sean was caught, convicted and sent to prison for three years. But Max's nightmares persisted. As the time approached for Sean to be released, Claire grew anxious. She approached her local Citizens Advice Bureau, which referred her to the local Mediation and Reparation Service. The mediators visited Sean who had just been released. He was surprised and upset to hear that his victims were still frightened. A meeting was arranged at a community centre. Sean apologised in full and reassured Claire he had no intention of burgling her house again. Claire accepted the apology and reassurance, and found the meeting helpful. Max's nightmares stopped soon afterwards.

Resolving sensitive issues

Restorative justice deals successfully with the often blurred distinction between offenders and victims. With young men in a fight, or warring neighbours, for example, it is not always clear who is the offender and who the victim. Under such circumstances, a criminal prosecution is not the best way to resolve that conflict. We can all be human and inhuman, violent and yet vulnerable and remorseful. We may at one moment be callous and insensitive but then become aware of and regret the damage we have caused. Mediation can address these ambiguities.

Another area where restorative justice may be helpful (with safeguards) is in the complex situations around violence in the home, such as domestic violence and child abuse. Often these are not reported because the criminal justice process may be perceived as making things worse. The collective shame and overall experience of bringing such cases to court is so damaging to the victims and the rest of the family that most such abuse is suffered in silence. Even if they succeed in gaining a conviction, the family is torn apart, and the victims are often left feeling more guilt than the offender.[18]

17 S. Braithwaite and M. Liebmann, *Restorative Justice – Does It Work?* (Bristol, Mediation UK, 1998), pp. 11–17.
18 Frances Rickford and Clare Dyer, *The Guardian*, G2, 29 November 1999, p. 8.

Restorative justice can address these sensitive issues. In Canada mediation and Family Group Conferences are increasingly used in just such difficult cases. In these settings, the victim and offender are surrounded by other family members and friends, and feel safe enough to raise and air their concerns. The proceedings are supported and managed by trained mediators, and consider the opinions of professionals such as social workers, doctors and teachers. But control rests with those who have been affected.[19]

---

19 Although this can have its drawbacks too. For example, in Native Canadian settlements in Northern Ontario, elders often sit in on circle sentencing sessions concerned with sex abuse cases which may have involved other elders. Women victims find this very difficult.

Chapter 5

The Offender

Mediation is seen by many justice professionals as a soft option for offenders. But often offenders find the process much harder than a court appearance, as they have to face up to their actions and to their victims. This needs an open environment where everything can be expressed – and heard. To help this to happen, mediation sessions usually have a few basic ground rules – such as no interruptions, and no violence. These are explained and agreed at the start.

Mediation encourages offenders to:
- own the responsibility for their crime
- become more aware of the effect of their crime on the victim
- reassess their future behaviour in the light of this knowledge
- apologise and/or offer appropriate reparation.[20]

The role of shame in criminal justice has recently been the subject of some interesting research. Being arrested, charged and appearing in court are all shameful experiences for most people, and are often felt to be punishments in themselves. This shame can be crippling, and often separates and stigmatises the accused as different from the rest of us. Offenders may then feel they are outcasts – and are often treated as such – and no longer feel part of society. Continued offending is the result.

John Braithwaite, an influential Australian criminologist, argues that shaming is a more effective sanction for unacceptable behaviour than other more overt forms of punishment – but only if it does not impose rejection and stigma. Shame must work to

---

20 Mediation UK, *Victim Offender Mediation Guidelines for Starting a Service* (Bristol, Mediation UK, 1993), p. 1.

reintegrate the offender into the community rather than exclude them permanently. He calls this 'reintegrative shaming'.[21]

Braithwaite noticed that crime is low in societies where shame is important but does not lead to the offender being cast out. He drew on Aboriginal experience and helped the spread of restorative justice in Australia and New Zealand. Thus shame can be a key ingredient for change where restorative justice is used, provided that it seeks to reintegrate the offender back into the community.

Assessing the value of mediation to offenders

Although many offenders find meeting their victims a daunting prospect, research on their attitudes after mediation has shown positive results. In the Umbreit and Roberts research in 1996 in Coventry and Leeds, 90% of offenders were satisfied with the outcome, and said it was important to apologise to the victim.[22] In the MARVEL Mediation Service for young offenders in 1997, 90% of offenders were satisfied or very satisfied with the service, and 91% would recommend it to a friend. In the SACRO scheme in Aberdeen in 1996–7, this figure was 87%.[23]

Moreover reparation and compensation that has been agreed through mediation has more chance of being completed, because offenders understand why it is needed. In the Northamptonshire Diversion Unit in 1994–5, 93% of compensation was paid after being agreed through mediation, compared with 48% of compensation ordered by the Inner London Youth Court.[24]

Reoffending

It is much more difficult to research the effect of restorative justice on recidivism. Despite the confidence with which politicians and media cite crime statistics, the measurement of reoffending is a

---

21 J. Braithwaite, *Crime, Shame and Reintegration* (Cambridge, Cambridge University Press, 1989).
22 M. Umbreit and A. Roberts, *Mediation of Criminal Conflict in England: An assessment of services in Coventry and Leeds* (St Paul, MN, University of Minnesota, Center for Restorative Justice and Mediation, 1996), pp. 14 and 23.
23 S. Braithwaite and M. Liebmann, *Restorative Justice – Does It Work?* (Bristol, Mediation UK, 1997), pp. 11–17.
24 *Ibid.* pp. 9–10.

very inexact science: reconvictions depend on effective police and court work, and self-reporting is itself inherently unreliable. This kind of research also takes a long time, and the resources are rarely available.

However, the research that has been done is cautiously encouraging. Research at the Leeds Victim-Offender Unit in 1997 showed a reconviction rate of 46.6% for those that had undertaken mediation, compared with a predicted reconviction rate of 54.2%. In the US, 41% of offenders in Umbreit's survey committed less serious crimes after mediation compared with 12% who had no mediation.[25] In New Zealand, research shows statistically significant lower reconviction rates and reduced seriousness of offences among those who have gone through restorative justice processes.[26] *No* studies have shown an *increase* in offending.

Currently both the Home Office in Britain and the National Institute of Justice in the US are doing further research in this area. Much hangs on the outcome. If restorative justice is shown to reduce reoffending, there are plans to promote its use widely. But if the research shows no such effect, there is the danger that restorative justice will be relegated once more to the margins of the justice system.

On the other hand, many exponents insist that restorative justice should not be judged just as a deterrent to future offending, but rather as a more civilised and positive response to the harm caused by crime. Even the offer of mediation improves the impression of the justice system for those caught up in it. Umbreit's research suggests that three-quarters of the victims and offenders offered mediation had a higher regard for their judicial process than those not offered the option. This positive impression included those who did not take up the offer.

Nevertheless, we must have realistic expectations. Mediation is a fairly short process, and while it can provide the motivation to change, much more is needed for many offenders to change their lives. Much as one might wish otherwise, Jason (see Chapter 1)

25 *Ibid.* pp. 7–8, and M. Umbreit, *Victim Meets Offender: The impact of restorative justice and mediation* (Monsey, NY, Criminal Justice Press, 1994).
26 Gabrielle Maxwell, Allison Morris and Tracy Anderson, *Community Panel Adult Pre-trial Diversion: Supplemetary evaluation* (Wellington, New Zealand, Crime Prevention Unit and Institute of Criminology, 1999).

was not ready to stop crime altogether. It was the only way of life he knew. Many of his friends are deeply into crime themselves. He has no job, nor skills, nor other support system.

Robert's story

Robert was 15 when he set fire to his school one night, causing £26,000 worth of damage and putting the school library out of action for several weeks. He had told his parents he was staying with a friend, so he walked through the night and returned home in the morning. He remained undetected until he walked into the local police station six days later to 'get something off his chest'. At first the police did not believe him, as he had not come to their attention before in any way.

When asked why he had set fire to the library, he said he had been worried about his forthcoming exams, and he thought that disrupting the library (where the exams took place) might buy him more time to revise. He had given himself up as he began to realise the harm he had caused and was consumed with guilt and remorse.

He was excluded from school while he waited for the Crown Court case, where (some months later) he was sentenced to two years at a Young Offender Institution. There he struggled to survive, being ridiculed and bullied for giving himself up to the police. Robert's parents felt he needed help, not incarceration. Robert himself wanted the chance to explain to the school why he had acted as he did.

A local youth restorative justice project contacted the head teacher of the school to see if he was interested in meeting with Robert and his family. He was keen to do so, as he had many questions to ask, and wanted to talk to Robert himself. The head teacher also wanted Robert to know that the school had not wanted him to go to prison and had written a letter of reference for him at court.

Robert's parents were also struggling to come to terms with what had happened. They wondered what the school thought of them as parents, and wanted the chance to express their support of the school.

After numerous visits and discussions, a Family Group Conference was convened at the school. Robert was given special leave from the prison to attend, and his parents and one of Robert's friends were there. The school was represented by the head teacher.

The conference lasted over two hours. Robert talked about what he had done, and his parents listened. Then they too had a chance to *say how they had been affected. Everyone was able to ask questions of each other. Robert spoke about how he wanted to take responsibility for what he had done, how he loved his family and regretted how he had hurt them as well as the school. At its conclusion, the head teacher took Robert to see the library, by now completely rebuilt. He wanted to show Robert that the scars on the building had been healed.*

Chapter 6

The Community

As described in Chapter 3, the notion that crime damages the wider community has informed the British criminal justice system for a millennium. It follows that the community is itself important in determining the credibility of sentences.

Often the media claim to speak for the community's views, though they may take a large part in forming those views by telling people what to think about harsh or soft sentences. Occasionally tabloid newspapers raise public petitions to have sentences shortened, but more often they attack the courts for being too soft.

In a recent Home Office study of attitudes to sentencing,[27] respondents said that sentences were generally too short, but when asked to suggest appropriate sentences for particular crimes, they consistently proposed sentences shorter than or similar to those actually given by the court. This matches the experience of sentencing exercises held by the Magistrates' Association up and down the country with diverse members of the public.[28]

People's needs vary widely in different communities. They are shaped by economic and social factors, by power and social status, by gender, generation, race and reputation. Moreover, community distribution of crime is very unequal. On estates where crime is high, it is a symptom of other problems:

- High levels of poverty; more than half of families living on state benefits
- High unemployment across three generations

27 Chris Nuttall, former Director of Home Office Research and Statistics.
28 Rosemary Thompson, former Chair of the Magistrates' Association.

- Many lone-parent households, with several children under 10
- Few play and leisure facilities
- A struggling local economy
- Physical isolation.

Two thousand neighbourhoods in the UK match these criteria as is reflected in their experience of crime:

- Crime rates three to four times higher than surrounding areas
- High levels of repeat victimisation
- Disorder and anti-social behaviour by youth
- Neighbourhood disputes and anti-social behaviour by adults
- Drug-dealing and prostitution.[29]

In such areas, the authorities are often seen as the enemy. Social workers who intend to help are seen only as people who take children into care. Police are those who arrest husbands and sons. Housing departments arrange evictions, or install difficult families next door. Water, gas and electricity companies are there to switch off the supply. Although by no means all of the families living on such estates are anti-social, there is often a collective stigma attached to them.

The word 'community' suggests a unity of purpose and identity which belies the social and ethnic diversity of most high-crime neighbourhoods. These are often characterised by short-term occupancy, irregular and sudden movement in and out of refugees, homeless families, illegal immigrants, ex-offenders and people released from mental hospitals, all of whom are themselves extremely vulnerable to victimisation.

However, even within such social mosaics – in North Kensington, in London, for example, local police deal with at least 37 different language groups – there are cohesive elements. Extended families, groups of refugees and immigrants, residents and religious groupings can all provide the basis for group participation in restorative justice encounters.

---

29 John Harding, Chief Probation Officer, Inner London Probation Service.

The use of mediation

Community participation in restorative justice is one of its corner-stones. It is fairly easy to imagine this working well in its original tribal settings, or its equivalent in isolated reservations. It is more of a challenge to integrate those principles into the diverse communities of inner cities in the UK. Tony Marshall, one of the long-term champions of mediation in the Home Office, set out the following restorative justice principles to achieve this:

1. Crime prevention depends on communities taking some responsibility for remedying the conditions that cause crime, not just leaving it to police.
2. The aftermath of crime cannot be fully resolved for the parties themselves *without their personal involvement*, be they victims, offenders, their families, or neighbours.
3. Justice measures must be flexible to respond to particular local exigencies, personal needs and potential for action.[30]

On the Meadowell estate in North Shields, alienated youth used to steal cars and joyride in races against the police. When one police chase went wrong, it led to the deaths of two popular local youths in a stolen car. Anti-police riots led to the burning of many shops and houses on the estate, including the recently built community centre, designed to provide activities for local youth but shut for three years because of local authority cuts.

After the riots of 1991, a new police strategy put local officers on the ground to listen closely to the needs and feelings of residents, and to respond by solving their problems. Their feelings were typical of many living in such situations: frustration at their powerlessness. This often expressed itself in fierce local disputes. Police were the enemy, so anyone who co-operated with them was labelled a 'grass', and their life made unbearable.

By listening and attempting to work through local issues, the local police officers provided an informal version of community and neighbourhood mediation, offering a way to restore power to such situations. Such work takes skilled and patient mediators, able to handle a diversity of temperaments and views. Often, in disputes over noise, vandalism, rowdy

30 Tony Marshall, *Restorative Justice: An overview* (London, Home Office, 1999), p. 6.

children and animals, both sides feel passionately that they are in the right. It takes diplomacy and tact to move them on to consider compromise as a success, not a defeat. Interestingly, the outcome of the Meadowell experiment was an increased reporting of crime by local people and a demand for a similar service from adjoining estates.

Many local community mediation services are involved in helping to resolve disputes in similar areas. The majority of neighbourhood disputes relate to noise: children playing football in the streets, music playing too loudly late at night. Nearly nine out of ten requests for assistance are accepted by mediation services. Eight out of ten are concluded (though not always successfully). One case in five is settled to the total satisfaction of all parties. But the process of talking together already represents a step forward from local war.[31]

31 Statistics from Mediation UK, 1996. They do not include the wide variety of informal police work in this area.

Chapter 7

What Choices are There?

This chapter sets out the established forms of restorative practice. In all cases a guilty plea is essential, or at least an acknowledgement of involvement, as mediation does not deal with the facts of guilt or innocence.[32] Most of these options can take place:
1. Before a trial
2. After conviction and before sentencing
3. During the period of the sentence – in prison or the community.

Restorative processes

Victim/offender mediation: indirect mediation
A trained mediator acts as a go-between, meeting the offender and victim separately to pass on concerns from one to the other. This can be an end in itself for parties reluctant to meet, or it can be the preliminary stage in arranging face-to-face mediation.

This 'shuttle diplomacy' can be time-consuming for mediators (and the agency which funds them). It may take several meetings before parties feel able to move forward. In Jason's case (see Chapter 1), his victim was too fearful to meet him, so his regret would have been passed to her through the mediator, as a message or in a personal letter.

Victim/offender mediation: face-to-face mediation
Arranging mediation between victims and offenders is a delicate matter. Often one party is willing but the other is not, for a host of

---

32 Sometimes offenders readily agree that they have committed a crime, but do not agree with the specific charge that is brought. So they may plead not guilty to the offence as charged, but be willing to acknowledge their responsibility in causing harm to the victim.

understandable reasons. Most practitioners of mediation insist that its voluntary nature is a key to its success. Neither party must be coerced into taking part.

Although many restorative justice practitioners believe that participation should be voluntary, I feel that even reluctant offenders would gain from mediation: meeting their victim promotes a sense of accountability missing from the impersonal setting of court. Victims can express their feelings, an opportunity not available in court, especially when a guilty plea means there is no trial.

In Britain and other European countries, mediation has been used mainly to deal with minor disputes and offences. But in some US states it is being increasingly used even for rape and murder. For instance, Texas Victims Services have used both indirect and direct mediation in dealing with the grief of the families of murder victims, who found their lives still damaged long after the court process was complete. I have filmed such scenes. Entering prison affects the victims deeply. Meeting their victim can profoundly touch the offender, marooned in the institutional world behind walls and bars. The following two examples show how mediation can work in very different situations.

Steve and Gilda

In 1984, Steve Figaroa was an angry, socially excluded teenager of 17. Following a drug deal that went wrong, he killed a young man and his innocent girlfriend Raynell. Steve was caught and convicted of first degree murder and sentenced to life. After 10 years in prison, he received a letter from Raynell's mother Gilda. She had been working with Texas Victims Services, trying unsuccessfully to come to terms with her loss. She wrote to Steve at their suggestion, so that some of the questions that were driving her to despair might be answered.

Over a year later, the Rev. David Doerfler of Texas Victims Services in Austin acted as a go-between, to see if a face-to-face meeting might be appropriate. In the end they met in prison, for a three-hour session. Steve explained the circumstances of the killing. Gilda told him of her feelings of continuing pain. This clearly was a shock to Steve, who had not considered her feelings for 10 years. When Gilda showed him pictures of her daughter, he wept and apologised.

Afterwards, Gilda told us she was unsure whether Steve had changed as a result of the mediation, but that it might be the start of forgiveness for her. More extraordinary still, Steve and Gilda now speak together to young offenders in prison, on the dangers of drugs and guns.

Emily and Sarah

Emily was referred to the Youth Offending Team after being warned by the police for making a threatening phone call to Sarah, a former close friend at school. An assessment visit made by mediators revealed that there were tensions at home between Emily and her parents. She had stopped attending school and was now 16, but with little idea of what she wanted to do next. Emily had resented Sarah for years, since their childhood friendship turned sour. She had been drinking one evening when she started talking about her feelings with her mates and made the call.

Emily was considering apologising to Sarah, but wanted to meet her to talk things through. The mediators contacted Sarah and her parents and arranged to visit. Sarah agreed to a meeting and the young women talked at length about their previous friendship and how it had broken down. It was clear that Emily had been badly affected by her feelings of rejection. She apologised to Sarah and assured her there would be no repeat of the phone call.

Following the mediation Emily completed a short course on job-seeking skills and embarked on a programme with the Prince's Trust. Her parents expressed their gratitude for the contact that Emily had with mediators and felt that the meeting had helped her move on from an emotional rut that she had been stuck in for years.

Victim/offender conferencing

Victim/offender conferencing follows similar restorative justice principles but involves more people. It brings together victims, offenders, their families and supporters, and relevant professionals – to talk and ask questions about the offence, and to make a plan to put things right and to prevent further offending. When this process involves a private planning time for the young person and their family it is called Family Group Conferencing.

Robin

Robin, aged 17, had been in and out of trouble for three years, with offences of theft from a car, theft from shops and four burglaries. He had fallen out with his family because of his offending, and was living in the home of one of his friends whose parents had decided to help him.

The local Intensive Support and Supervision Programme arranged a
Family Group Conference using an independent co-ordinator. In the end
15 people attended: Robin, his mother, father and sister; his friend and his
parents, and an uncle; his foster mother who had looked after him at one
point; his social worker, a police officer, a Youth Offending Team officer, a
Victim Support worker (the victims did not want to come themselves) and
a volunteer mentor. Robin took on board the statements made by the
Victim Support worker about the effects of burglary on victims, which he
had not realised before. The plan formulated by the conference centred
round Robin making a home with his friend's family and getting a job.
A year later he was still managing to keep out of trouble.

Victim/offender mediation: victim/offender groups

Some people are too frightened to meet their own victim or
offender but still wish to express their feelings. Many victims of
crime never meet their offenders, either because they have not
been caught, or because when caught they refuse to participate.
Victim/offender groups help victims to meet other offenders who
have committed similar crimes. For example, Jason would be able
to find out from other victims what the impact of burglary had
been on them, while his victim could meet and express her anger
to other burglars.

In 1985, in Rochester, Kent, Victims and Offenders in Conciliation (VOIC)
brought groups of four to six victims of burglaries together with convicted
young burglars aged between 15 and 20. Victims of crime were found
through the local Victim Support Scheme. Offenders volunteered to take
part. The groups met at the Youth Custody Centre for three sessions of one
and a half hours, at weekly intervals. Afterwards, victims felt less anxious;
they had found the offenders more friendly than they had anticipated.
Offenders rated victims more highly, and understood the emotional
implications of burglary on their victims much better.[33]

Victim/offender mediation: surrogate victim

Occasionally there is an opportunity for a victim and an offender of
similar crimes to meet on an individual rather than on a group basis.

33 G. Launay, 'Bringing victims and offenders together: A comparison of two models' in
Howard Journal, 23 (3), 1985, pp. 200–12, cited in M. Wright, *Justice for Victims and Offenders*,
2nd edn (Winchester, Waterside Press, 1996), pp. 122–3.

Susan

Susan, an active young mother, lived in a terraced house that was burgled. This affected her badly. She had difficulty sleeping, and suspected all strangers, including people at the bus stop outside her house. She watched them obsessively, and called the police at the slightest sign of unusual behaviour. Susan was helped by Victim Support, but still worried about why her house had been chosen. A probation officer arranged a meeting between Susan and her husband and Martin, a burglar from another case who wanted to apologise to his victims, but had been unable to do so.

They met in prison, where Martin was serving three years for two burglaries. Susan asked many questions, and felt reassured by Martin's answers. He seemed genuinely concerned about what had happened to her. After the meeting, Susan slept well, and returned to normal, a great relief to her husband and children. She only wished that the meeting had taken place earlier. Martin was pleased to help a victim similar to his. He could now concentrate on his studies, preparing for a straight life on release.

Where mediation is not suitable

Medition is not suitable for all situations. Safety is paramount for both victim and offender. Mediators assess this by visiting both sides first. If there is any doubt about safety, or if the mediation seems likely to cause harm – for instance if the offender's attitude to the victim is very negative – the case is not accepted. Sometimes indirect mediation can be carried out instead, such as a letter of apology. Sexual offences and domestic violence are areas where many are wary of mediation. It is generally accepted that mediation in such cases should take place at the initiative of the victim, who should be able to receive counselling. Offenders should also undertake work on victim awareness before mediation.

Restorative outcomes

Compensation through the courts

This takes the form of cash repayments to the victim, for theft or damage to property, if the offender has the resources. However, it is often paid in irregular instalments and seldom in full, leaving victims frustrated and having to pursue the payments through civil action, if they think it is worth it. But compensation agreed through mediation is nearly always paid, because offenders understand what the money is needed for. In the US there have been some attempts to create work for young people so that they can pay compensation to victims.

One imaginative scheme in Lincoln, Nebraska, involves local businesses in funding the YMCA to pay for jobs for convicted young people, so that they can repay their victims. This also teaches the reality of working for money, and raises employers' awareness of offenders' lives and problems.

Direct reparation to victims: practical work

Sometimes mediation can identify a practical way of making amends to the victim, like removing graffiti, or mending broken fences and windows. For instance, some shops which have been victims of shoplifting have asked their offenders to work for them to repay their debt, and see the impact of what they have done.

Tim was given a six-hour Reparation Order for causing criminal damage to the boundary fence of a local health centre. After discussions and apologies, Tim expressed his willingness to try and put things right with some practical work. It was not possible for him to do this at the health centre because of client confidentiality, so arrangements were made for Tim to paint over some graffiti at another public building.

Direct reparation to victims: apologies and symbolic reparation

Many victims feel an apology is more important than tangible reparation. It is important that this apology is sincere, otherwise victims may feel offenders are apologising just to look good or because they feel it is expected.

Reparation need not be direct repair of harm done. Many offenders are unable to compensate their victims for the value of all the goods they have stolen or damaged. Sometimes the actual damage has already been repaired by the time the offender is caught. But reparation can take symbolic form, such as a letter of apology, bunch of flowers or box of chocolates. Even small gifts such as these can be a large expense to a young offender with no money.

I filmed a mediation dealing with the damage a young boy had caused to a garage owner's precious motorbike. The victim was furious, and initially refused to meet the boy and his family. But the mediator helped the victim to tell the lad how much the bike meant to him, and how angry he was. The boy's father was also ashamed and angry. The boy was dismayed that a prank he had done as a dare had caused such distress. The victim was moved to accept his apology. After the session, he gave the lad a ride on the back of his bike, and promised to teach him motor mechanics.

Reparation to the community

This is a symbolic repayment to the wider community. It is often requested by victims who want nothing for themselves. It was also established through Community Service Orders, which courts have been imposing for many years. Such work can but does not need to be related to the crime.

In South London, convicted burglars have used their knowledge to put locks on the flats of elderly people. Others have worked in old people's homes or with children who have learning disabilities.

For some young people, this reparation may be the first time they have been valued by outsiders, and their first contribution to the community. If young offenders feel motivated and satisfied at doing something positive, they may in time be able to give up the prestige and excitement of crime.

Stewart was a persistent young offender I knew from his Intensive Probation Order at Sherborne House in London. He stole cars. His father, a violent man with a long criminal record, beat him regularly. Stewart's 10 weeks at Sherborne House provided him with positive activities like sport and metalwork. On his Community Service, he worked with injured animals. He found caring for animals brought out a tenderness he had not realised was there. Afterwards he found a job in a veterinary supplies shop, where his employers found him to be a responsible and energetic employee.

Action plans

Mediation with victims may prompt offenders to a change of heart. But to sustain their commitment to change, some restorative justice procedures address the wider issues that lead youngsters into crime.

The French Juges des Enfants stage mediation sessions in their chambers with young offenders, their parents and the victim and their family. They explore why the crime happened and what would prevent it happening again. The Juge can order local authorities to act on housing or education recommendations that may emerge from those sessions.

In Britain, Action Plans to be drawn up by the new Youth Offending Teams are based on the successful experience of Northamptonshire Diversion Schemes in the 1980s for adults and young people. In Northamptonshire, a multi-disciplinary group of police, probation officers, social workers and other trained mediators responded to cases referred to them by local police which could be suitable for a caution, providing the offender accepted their guilt. Indirect mediation was initiated, which sometimes led to face-to-face mediation. This could result in an apology from the offender and in other ways of making good the harm done. When this process was completed, the offender's action plan became part of the caution by the police. Action plans could include, for instance, an apology to the victim, appropriate reparation, attendance at an alcohol education group, seeking careers advice, and the like.[34]

---

34 For young people, the Crime and Disorder Act 1998 has now replaced cautions by reprimands and final warnings.

Chapter 8

Current Services

At what stage in the criminal justice process can mediation be used?

Mediation and reparation schemes can function at *all* stages of the criminal justice process, taking into account different factors at each stage. Most of these options are available to all offenders and victims, except those specified by legislation for young offenders, such as Reparation Orders under the Crime and Disorder Act 1998.

1. **Community**: some incidents can be treated as *community matters instead of crimes*. For instance, a school fight could result in the police being called or be resolved by school-based mediation. In the case of disturbances involving young people (or adults) the police can either make arrests or ask their local community mediation service to sort out the conflict.

2. **Pre-prosecution:** some schemes *divert offenders from court.* Until recently, such schemes were usually organised by Juvenile Liaison Bureaux as part of police cautions to keep young offenders from court. From June 2000, when the Crime and Disorder Act of 1998 came into force, cautions have been replaced by 'reprimands' (first offence) and 'final warnings' (second offence), at which point the young offender must be referred to the local Youth Offending Team (YOT). YOTs are encouraged to offer victim/offender mediation or conferencing, if everyone concerned is willing. Adults who are cautioned (but not prosecuted) can be referred to a local mediation service, where there is one.

3. **Court-based, pre-conviction:** these schemes offer *mediation before proceedings*. In England and Wales the prosecutor or court can discontinue (but not defer) a case in its preliminary stages and recommend mediation. However, so far this power has seldom been used. In Scotland, the Procurator Fiscal may actually defer cases for mediation, provided they are serious enough to go to court.

4. **Court-based, post-conviction:** mediation can take place *after conviction but before sentence*. Although used often, critics argue that this invites false remorse on tactical grounds, and puts pressure on the victim to accept it.

5. **During the sentence:** mediation can happen *during the sentence itself* (see Steve and Gilda's story, page 43). This can be in addition to probation or community service, or during a prison sentence. The Crime and Disorder Act has in fact introduced new sentences, such as Reparation Orders and Action Plan Orders which can include opportunities for mediation.

6. **After completion of sentence:** mediation can take place *after a sentence has been completed*. It is thus additional to the sentence. Some see this as unfair but it often promotes closure not provided by conventional justice.

Funding for Services

Probation-led and voluntary sector services take different forms, but have similar aims. They provide communication between a victim and an offender using a trained mediator, sometimes a member of staff, often a trained member of the community. Mediators are either volunteers or paid a sessional fee. This is a particularly good way for community members to become involved constructively in law and order issues. Martin Wright believes that projects are influenced by their source of funding, as well as by the kinds of cases they handle.[35]

35 M. Wright, *Justice for Victims and Offenders*, 2nd edn (Winchester, Waterside Press, 1996), pp. 84–5.

Private or charitable funding promotes an image of neutrality. The parties do not generally feel as stigmatised by bringing problems to a service funded in this way, as opposed to a court, police or probation mediation service. Local people are usually involved in management; but such projects may have trouble attracting cases unless good relationships can be developed with police and courts. Also, long-term funding is scarce.

Funding from government agencies (local or national) helps to secure referrals, but these services sometimes try too hard to make people attend. Success may be seen as easing pressure on the system rather than meeting the needs of individuals. In fact, it does both.

Agencies involved in victim/offender mediation

Many agencies have been involved in victim/offender mediation and have played an important part in promoting it.

Victim Support
In the early days of victim/offender mediation in the UK in the early 1980s, Victim Support took the lead, organising seminars and working parties, and helping people and organisations to come together to form a mediation organisation, which later became Mediation UK.

Police
Many of the early schemes in the UK were started by police and social service youth justice teams, usually as a way of diverting young offenders from prosecution. Most of these early projects did not survive.

However, police interest was rekindled by the work of Sergeant Terry O'Connell in New South Wales, Australia, in the early 1990s. O'Connell had been inspired by the use of restorative justice in New Zealand and had adapted the Family Group Conferences to his police work, establishing the police role as central to the Australian model of conferencing. Although some critics object to the police acting as mediators, there are now police-run schemes in Canada, Australia and Tasmania, the UK and the US.

In the UK, restorative justice was given a significant boost in the early 1990s by Chief Superintendent Caroline Nicholl of the Thames Valley Police, a progressive thinker in police circles. She arranged for first-time juvenile shoplifters in Milton Keynes to meet local shopkeepers to discuss the impact of what may have seemed to them a minor, victimless crime.

The success of this experiment convinced many sceptical local police officers of the efficacy of restorative justice. This opinion was reinforced by a tour of the UK by Terry O'Connell in 1994, and subsequent visits. The Thames Valley Chief Constable, Charles Pollard, was inspired to promote the use of conferencing for offenders, victims and their families, facilitated by police on O'Connell's model. A special unit was set up in 1998, and training established on a major scale. Police in Surrey and Nottinghamshire have followed suit. Thames Valley Police have also started to use conferencing in internal discipline cases, and for complaints against police – both areas that need a better way to be resolved.

The probation service
The first victim/offender mediation service in the UK was started by South Yorkshire Probation Service in 1983, and three of the four schemes funded by the Home Office in 1985–7 were run by the probation service. The probation service in these areas has continued to fund these schemes, and they have become centres of excellence, with 15 years' experience in the field. Like the police, some probation officers are doubtful, but those who have done it become advocates of mediation.

Social services and children's charities
A few local social services have run victim/offender mediation services, sometimes in partnership with voluntary agencies. Several of the larger children's charities have started victim/offender mediation services themselves, such as Barnardos and NCH (formerly National Children's Home). These are for cases involving young people under 18.

Community mediation services
Once they are well established, community mediation services often expand their remit to include school and victim/offender

mediation. Some mediation services have included community and victim/offender mediation alongside each other from the start.

Multi-agency teams

In several areas victim/offender mediation has been undertaken by multi-agency teams of professionals. The most well-known of these was the Northamptonshire Diversion Unit, which was formed with staff seconded from the police, probation and social services, youth, education and health services.

This model has been used as the basis for recent government legislation under the 1998 Crime and Disorder Act to set up multi-agency Youth Offending Teams. About 45 of these new teams have received funds from the Youth Justice Board to establish restorative justice schemes involving young offenders and their victims. This will double the number of restorative justice services in the UK.

Chapter 9

New Government Legislation

Young offenders

There are two major new pieces of legislation which will influence the development of restorative justice in England and Wales (and possibly be extended to Northern Ireland and Scotland). They are both concerned with young people, and reflect the Labour government's policy of prioritising the fight against youth crime.

Crime and Disorder Act 1998

This legislation specifies that young offenders will be ordered to undertake reparation to the victim or community. There is a growing consensus that the legislation will work best for both victims and offenders if it is implemented through restorative processes.[36] The Act specifies the formation of multi-disciplinary Youth Offending Teams (police, probation, social services, health and education services, plus optional partnerships with the voluntary sector) to share resources in working with offenders to reduce reoffending.

Final warning
Replacing the multiple caution, this is usually given for a second minor offence, following a reprimand for a first minor offence. After a final warning, the young person must be referred to the Youth Offending Team (YOT) for a rehabilitation programme to prevent reoffending. This can include victim awareness work, mediation, conferencing or reparation (or all of these).

---

36 See S. Braithwaite and M. Liebmann, *Restorative Justice – Does It Work?* (Bristol, Mediation UK, 1998).

Reparation Order

This requires young offenders to make reparation to the victim or to the community. It can involve up to 24 hours' work and must be completed within three months. It does not include monetary compensation. Victim awareness work, mediation and reparation work can all count towards the hours of a Reparation Order. The Order should specify the names of victims to receive reparation and should be based on a report prepared by the Youth Offending Team. However, this puts great time pressure on the process, so in some areas courts specify the number of hours, and the mediation service explores the possibilities afterwards; this allows time for victims to consider whether they would like direct reparation, or whether community reparation is more appropriate. It also allows for changes of activity where necessary.

Action Plan Order

This Order requires a young offender to follow an action plan for three months, which can include a variety of activities designed to prevent further offending, such as attending an alcohol dependence group, advice on drugs or help with literacy. These activities are specified in the Order and can also include appropriate reparative work, such as victim awareness, mediation, conferencing or reparation. A Family Group Conference is a very good way of planning the content of the Order.

Supervision Order

A Supervision Order provides for supervision of a young offender for a period of time (often one or two years). These Orders have existed for many years, but the Crime and Disorder Act makes provision for them to include reparation where appropriate.

Youth Justice and Criminal Evidence Act 1999

Referral Order

Part 1 of this Act introduces a new sentence for 10–17 year olds pleading guilty and convicted for the first time. It involves referral of the young person to a Youth Offender Panel, which meets in an informal setting away from the court. The people involved in this meeting are the young person, their family, the victims if they wish (but there is no pressure to attend), a member of the YOT (which is responsible for preparations for the meeting) and two panel members drawn from the local community (and provided with training for this work). One of them chairs the panel meeting. Other relevant people may also attend, such as a teacher from the young person's school.

The meeting considers the circumstances leading to the offending behaviour and the effect of the crime on the victim. The panel then agrees a contract with the young person, including reparation to the victim or to the wider community, and a programme of activity designed primarily to prevent further offending. The aim of the Referral Order is for the young person to accept responsibility for their offending behaviour and to consider – along with those with a positive influence over the young person – how to deal with the causes. The offence becomes 'spent' as soon as the Order has been completed.

This process has many similarities with Family Group Conferences and also draws on experiences of the Scottish Children's Hearings for young offenders and other vulnerable youth. It is the first explicitly restorative legislation in the UK in terms of both victim and offender. Pilot schemes started in seven areas of England and Wales in July 2000 and will be evaluated by three universities, with a view to making the provisions available across England and Wales from early 2002.[37]

Adult offenders

Although both these new provisions apply only to young people from 10 to 17, those involved in restorative justice hope that, if all goes well, there will be similar or parallel provisions for adults. The fact that the government has commissioned research into established mediation services for adults is a positive sign.

---

37 Home Office and Youth Justice Board, *The Referral Order: Draft guidance to youth offending teams* (London, Home Office and Youth Justice Board, January 2000).

Chapter 10

The Future

A number of restorative provisions have been established for some years now, such as Victim Support, Compensation Orders and Criminal Injuries Compensation. Mediation and conferencing are newer, and research into the effects of mediation on both victims and offenders is ongoing. But such effects as have been reported are at best consistently positive – and at worst no less effective than retributive justice. Given the generally negative culture of the latter, and its greater cost, the case for extending restorative justice initiatives is strong.

There are many ways in which restorative justice is moving into British institutions. In some places it is becoming well established, in others it is patchy or piecemeal. Restorative justice processes should be available everywhere, so that all who want to use them have this choice. The following examples show some of the applications and possibilities, but the field is growing so rapidly that it cannot be a complete list.

Community and schools

Many offences are already tackled within the community. If there is a serious fight in a school playground, often the school deals with it, involving the parents as well as the students. Usually students are suspended, and sometimes expelled. Occasionally the police may be called. If there is a school peer mediation service, there is a possibility of sorting things out in a more restorative way.

In some towns and cities in the UK, police work together with the local community mediation service to resolve community conflict without bringing criminal charges. All concerned meet to deal with the cause of the problem rather than arresting people again and again.

In Austria, if reparation is made through mediation before the offence is notified to the police, *no crime is deemed to have been committed*. If the victim is not interested in reparation, or cannot be traced, reparation can be made to a charitable fund or through community service.

Criminal courts

It would be possible for courts to offer victims the option of mediation or a conference for many adult and juvenile offences prior to trial – and instead of it – especially for minor offences or cases arising from private disputes. This already happens in some courts in Scotland, France, Germany and Canada.

In Winnipeg, Canada, some 900 cases a year are first referred to the local voluntary mediation service by the Crown Prosecution Service. The disputants in such cases as fights have an hour to agree an acceptable resolution, and any reparation. This must be accepted as fair by the bench. If the disputants fail to agree, the case comes to trial.

Thus court cases could be limited to those that cannot be settled through mediation and reparation, or are so serious or complex that they need to be dealt with in public.

In a poll of 4,400 people in Hamburg, Germany, many wanted a wide range of offences to be dealt with away from court – directly by the parties themselves, or with a third party as mediator. Moreover, using a fictitious case of theft of DM 1,000, three out of four said they would urge the judge to impose restitution as the sentence. Only one in 10 chose punishment exclusively. For the vast majority of petty crimes, the same proportion backed restitution through mediation. Only burglary and rape were deemed necessary to be punished in court, and only rape was widely agreed to be inappropriate for the use of restitution.[38]

As Martin Wright has shown, this is not far-fetched. In Britain, the Inland Revenue and Customs and Excise already only go to court in serious or persistent cases, or if the offence is denied. Resolution of other offences is agreed privately between the agency and offenders.

---

38 Klaus Sessar, 'Restitution or punishment: An empirical study on attitudes of the public and the justice system in Hamburg' in *Eurocriminology*, 8–9, 1995, pp. 199–214.

Using this model for other criminal offences, prosecution would proceed only when adequate reparation is not voluntarily forthcoming from the offender. Some German courts already do this, working out an agreement between defence, prosecution and the offender, overseen by a probation officer who reports the completion of the reparation to the bench. This spares the state the expense of a court case and the offender a criminal record.

For those cases which need to go to court, mediation could be offered at a later stage, depending on the victim's wishes. This might be before sentencing (and the court could either ignore the mediated agreement or take it into account). It would be more likely after sentencing, when mediation or a conference would offer victim and offender a chance to deal with issues not covered in the court case.

Prisons and after

Prison is a traumatic experience for inmates and their families. Families are left bereft while prisoners have a host of unresolved and unasked questions which are never dealt with in the painful setting of occasional visits. When prisoners come out, often to nothing, their return to family life can be deeply disruptive for all concerned. It often leads to a return to crime. Mediation and Family Group Conferencing could be used to resolve these problems. They could also help to deal with unresolved issues for victims, such as fear of repeat victimisation if the offender moves back to their area.

Restorative processes could also be used for many difficult situations inside prisons: discipline proceedings for inmates and staff, and for conflicts between inmates. Some prisons are already beginning to explore this.

Unsolved crimes: the victims' needs

The largest problem with mediation, as with other forms of justice, is that most crimes remain unsolved, rendering them out of reach of court or restorative procedures. That leaves many victims unfairly neglected. Susan Herman, Director of the National Center for Victims of Crime, Washington DC, proposes instead what she calls 'parallel justice', in which victims would have a hearing of their case, so that the pain they have been through would be acknowledged publicly, and appropriate remedial action taken. In the UK, this could be developed within a local crime prevention structure, or by extending the Criminal Injuries Compensation Authority to include a wider range of crimes. Depending on the individual, this can involve more longer term medical or social support – such as job retraining – than currently seen as 'damage' by the courts.[39]

Commercial and civil cases

With the encouragement of recent reforms of the civil courts (the 1999 Civil Procedure Rules), many more commercial disputes, such as over insurance claims, and other civil matters can be resolved by alternative dispute resolution (ADR). This is usually through arbitration or mediation. ADR can save huge amounts of time and money for all parties, and is considerably less stressful than going to court.

Institutions and businesses

Institutions and businesses could use mediation and conferencing to deal with internal tensions, complaints and disciplinary proceedings. Restorative justice might then become the normal paradigm instead of the apportioning of blame and resulting sanctions.

Organisations providing public services

Mediation and conferencing could be used in public service bodies for complaints against staff and in internal disciplinary proceedings. This is already happening in the health service for complaints against GPs and is being introduced by some police services. In areas where there has been public dissatisfaction with complaints systems, restorative processes provide a more open way of dealing with grievances.

Children at risk

Some welfare organisations and social service departments already use Family Group Conferences to involve family members with children at risk of going into care. The family and the conference often come up with imaginative plans which avoid such a drastic solution. Conferencing could be extended to other family crises, such as long-term illness or the care of elderly parents, so that families feel empowered to manage them wherever possible.

39 Susan Herman speaking at the International Symposium on Victimology, Montreal, Canada, 10 August 2000.

The importance of continued government support

The government has recognised the potential of restorative justice. But there is always the danger that it will not sustain its commitment and will fail to provide the resources for training and mediation services to become properly established across Britain – with the risk of schemes providing a poor service and allowing the principles of restorative justice to fall into disrepute. One particular risk in the UK is that the 1999 legislation for young people will concentrate all the restorative justice resources on them – losing the valuable experience of working with adult offenders, and restricting benefits for victims to those whose offenders are under 18.

This chapter suggests the wide role that mediation can play at every stage of the judicial process or even before it starts. Care will have to be taken to ensure quality of service. For this, government support is vital. As a long-term observer of the failure of the current justice system to deter, to deliver what both victims and offenders see as justice, or to satisfy the emotional needs of victims, I am impatient to see changes that are more than procedural adjustments.

Conclusion

It is well known that many people catch infections in hospital that they did not have before they went in. If we want to restore confidence in the justice system, we must ensure that victims and offenders are not more damaged by the process than they were by the crime. We also know that victims often want reassurance, explanations and apologies more than they want the offender to be punished.

As we enter the new millennium, we have a choice. We can remain trapped in the vicious circle of crime followed by punishment, followed by more crime and more punishment – or we can return to ancient principles of conflict resolution, and try to close the circle broken by crime. The overriding need is to reinvigorate the justice system and reconnect it to people and communities affected by crime. Restorative justice looks beyond offending to the common humanity that will hopefully bring offenders to grasp what they have done, to work to heal their victims, and so help both to rejoin their community.

Retributive and Restorative Justice: A Comparison

Retributive Justice	Restorative Justice
Crime defined as violation of the state	Crime defined as violation of one person by another
Focus on establishing blame, on guilt, on the past (did they do it?)	Focus on problem solving on liabilities and obligations in future (what should be done?)
Adversarial relationships and process	Dialogue and negotiation
Imposition of pain to punish and deter/prevent	Restitution as a means of restoring both parties: reconciliation/restoration as goal
Justice defined by intent and by process; right rules	Justice defined as right relationships; judged by the outcome
One social injury replaced by another	Focus on repair of social injury
Action directed from state to offender: – victim ignored – offender passive	Victim's and offender's roles recognised in both problem and solution – victim's rights/needs recognised – offender encouraged to take responsibility
Offender accountability defined as taking punishment	Offender accountability defined as understanding impact of action and helping decide how to make things right
Response focused on offender's past behaviour	Response focused on harmful consequences of offender's behaviour

From H. Zehr, *Retributive Justice, Restorative Justice: New perspectives on crimes and justice* (Elkhart, Indiana, Mennonite Central Committee on Criminal Justice, 1985).

Glossary

These definitions are based on documents published by Mediation UK and the Restorative Justice Consortium.[40]

Action Plan Order
An order that requires a young offender to follow an action plan for three months, which can include a variety of specified activities designed to prevent further offending.

Advocacy
An intervention or negotiation on behalf of another party.

Arbitration
A process in which an impartial third party makes a final, usually binding decision. The discussion and decision, while structured, may not be as tightly regulated by formal procedures and rules of evidence as is courtroom procedure.

Litigation
The process of deciding a dispute in court according to law, with advocates presenting evidence on behalf of the parties, or in some cases the parties acting for themselves. Litigation is an adversarial process, in which a judge or jury, after hearing both sides, adjudicates in favour of one party.

Mediation
A process by which an impartial third party helps two or more disputants work out how to resolve a conflict. The disputants, not the mediators, decide the terms of any agreement reached. Mediation usually focuses on future rather than past behaviour.

---

40 Mediation UK, *Training Manual in Community Mediation Skills* (Bristol, Mediation UK, 1995), p. 55; Mediation UK, *Victim Offender Mediation Guidelines for Starting a Service* (Bristol, Mediation UK, 1993), p. 2; SINRJ (Standards in Restorative Justice), *Standards for Restorative Justice* (London, Restorative Justice Consortium, 1999), p. 3.

Mediation (victim/offender)
A process in which victim(s) and offender(s) communicate with the help of an impartial third party, either directly, face to face, or indirectly via the third party. It enables victims to express their needs and feelings, and offenders to accept and act on their responsibilities.

Mediator
A person who helps two or more parties in a dispute (or a victim and an offender) to work towards a resolution. A mediator is impartial, is not directly involved in the dispute and has no stake in the outcome.

Negotiation
The process of disputants working out an agreement between themselves.

Offence
An act prohibited by the criminal law which has been reported to the police and recorded or proceeded upon.

Offender
A person who has admitted, takes responsibility for or has been convicted of an offence.

Probation Order
An order which provides supervision of an offender aged 16 or over, for a period of time (between six months and three years), by a probation officer.

Referral Order
An order which involves the referral of a young offender to a Youth Offender Panel, under the provisions of the Youth Justice and Criminal Evidence Act 1999.

Reparation
The contribution that can be made by the offender to the victim, to help put right the physical or emotional harm caused by the crime.

Reparation Order
An order that requires young offenders to make reparation to the victim or to the community. It can involve up to 24 hours' work and must be completed within three months. It does not include monetary compensation.

Restorative justice

Seeks to balance the concerns of the victim and the community with the need to reintegrate the offender into society. It also seeks to assist the recovery of the victim and enable all parties with a stake in the justice process to participate fruitfully in it.

Retributive justice

Aims to deliver a proportionate amount of punishment to an offender who has committed a crime. Victims have no part to play except as witnesses in cases where offenders plead not guilty.

Supervision Order

An order which provides supervision of a young offender aged 10 to 17, for a period of time (between six months and three years), by a social worker or probation officer.

Victim (of crime)

A person against whom an offence has been committed – also that person's family, friends, witnesses and others who have been affected by the crime.

Victim/offender groups

Groups where victims and offenders of similar crimes (e.g. burglary), but not of the actual crimes, can meet to discuss the impact of these crimes.

Victim Support

A national voluntary agency with a network of local schemes which provide emotional and practical support to victims of crime.

Youth Offender Panel

Forum where a young offender, the family, the victim (if appropriate), a member of the Youth Offending Team and two community panel members can consider the young person's offending behaviour and the effect of the crime on the victim. This leads to a contract with the young person to include reparation to the victim and a programme of activity to prevent further offending.

Youth Offending Team

Multi-disciplinary team of professionals (from police, probation, social, health and education services) sharing resources in working with young offenders to implement the Crime and Disorder Act 1998 and the Youth Justice and Criminal Evidence Act 1999.

Further Reading

Akester, K., *Restoring Youth Justice* (London, Justice, 2000).

Bazemore, G. and Walgrave, L. (eds), *Restorative Juvenile Justice: Repairing the harm of youth crime* (Monsey, NY, Willow Tree Press, 1999).

Braithwaite, J., *Crime, Shame and Reintegration* (Cambridge, Cambridge University Press, 1989)

Braithwaite, S. and Liebmann, M., *Restorative Justice – Does It Work?* (Bristol, Mediation UK, 1998).

Consedine, J., *Restorative Justice: Healing the effects of crime* (Lyttleton, New Zealand, Ploughshares Publications, 1995).

Galaway, B. and Hudson, J. (eds), *Restorative Justice: International perspectives* (Monsey, NY, Criminal Justice Press; and Amsterdam, Kugler, 1996).

Genn, H., *Mediation in Action: Resolving court disputes without trial* (London, Calouste Gulbenkian Foundation, 1999).

Graef, R., *Living Dangerously: Young offenders in their own words* (London, Fontana, 1993).

Home Office and Youth Justice Board, *The Referral Order: Draft guidance to youth offending teams* (London, Home Office and Youth Justice Board, January 2000).

Hudson, J., Morris, A., Maxwell, G. and Galaway, B., *Family Group Conferences: Perspectives on policy and practice* (Annandale, Australia, The Federation Press, 1996).

Liebmann, M. (ed.), *Mediation in Context* (London, Jessica Kingsley Publishers, 2000).

Marshall, T., *Restorative Justice: An overview* (London, Home Office, 1999).

Marshall, T. and Merry, S., *Crime and Accountability* (London, HMSO, 1990).

Mediation UK, *Practice Standards (for mediators and management of mediation services),* (Bristol, Mediation UK, 1998).

Mediation UK, *Victim Offender Mediation Guidelines for Starting a Service* (Bristol, Mediation UK, 1993).

Quill, D. and Wynne, J., *Victim and Offender Mediation Handbook* (London, Save the Children, 1993). Available from Mediation UK.

Roberts, A. and Masters, G., *Group Conferencing: Restorative justice in practice* (St Paul, MN, University of Minnesota, Center for Restorative Justice and Mediation, 1998). Fax: 612-625-8224, E-mail: rjp@tlcmail.che.umn.edu. Also available on Website: ssw.che.umn.edu/rjp.

Standards in Restorative Justice (SINRJ), *Standards for Restorative Justice* (London, Restorative Justice Consortium, 1999).

Stewart, S., *Conflict Resolution: A foundation guide* (Winchester, Waterside Press, 1997).

Umbreit, M., *Victim Meets Offender: The impact of restorative justice and mediation* (Monsey, NY, Criminal Justice Press, 1994).

Van Ness, D. and Strong, K.H., *Restoring Justice* (Cincinnati, OH, Anderson Publishing Co., 1997).

Wright, M., *Justice for Victims and Offenders,* 2nd edn (Winchester, Waterside Press, 1996).

Wright, M., *Restoring Respect for Justice* (Winchester, Waterside Press, 1999).

Youth Justice Board, *Guidance for the Development of Effective Restorative Practice with Young Offenders* (London, Home Office, 1999).

Zehr, H., *Changing Lenses: A new focus for criminal justice* (Scottsdale, PA, and Waterloo, Ontario, Herald Press, 1990). Available from London Mennonite Centre, 14 Shepherds Hill, Highgate, London N6 5AQ, Tel: 020 8340 8775, Fax: 020 8341 6807, E-mail: metanoia@menno.org.uk.

Some of the non-UK books in this section are available from Blackstone Press Ltd, Aldine Place, London W12 8AA, Tel: 020 8740 2277, Fax: 020 8743 2292, E-mail: sales@blackstone.demon.co.uk, Website: www.blackstonepress.com.

Organisations Involved in Restorative Justice

Crime Concern
89 Albert Embankment, London
SE1 7TS
Tel: 020 7587 5400
Fax: 020 7587 1617
E-mail:
enquiry@crimeconcern-se.org.uk
Website: www.crimeconcern.org.uk

Provides training and consultancy in
restorative practice and manages
victim/offender mediation and
reparation services.

**European Forum for Victim-
Offender Mediation and
Restorative Justice**
Hooverplein 10, 3000 Leuven,
Belgium
Tel: 00 32 16 32 54 29
Fax: 00 32 16 32 54 63
E-mail:
jolien.willemsens@law.kuleuven.ac.be

Helps to establish and develop victim/
offender mediation and other restorative justice practices throughout
Europe.

Justice
59 Carter Lane, London EC4V 5AQ
Tel: 020 7329 5100
Fax: 020 7329 5055
E-mail: admin@justice.org.uk

An all-party, legal human rights
organisation which aims to improve
British justice through law reform and
policy work, publications and training.

Mediation UK
Alexander House, Telephone Avenue,
Bristol BS1 4BS
Tel: 0117 904 6661
Fax: 0117 904 3331
E-mail: enquiry@mediationuk.org.uk
Website: www.mediationuk.org.uk

Umbrella organisation for many of
the victim/offender mediation services
in the UK.

NACRO
169 Clapham Road, London SW9 0PU
Tel: 020 7582 6500
Fax: 020 7735 4666
E-mail: rob.allen@nacro.org.uk
Website: www.nacro.org.uk

Runs and develops restorative justice
projects and provides training and
consultancy.

**National Center for Victims of
Crime**
2111 Wilson Blvd. Suite 300,
Arlington, VA 22201, USA
Tel: 001 703 276 2880
Fax: 001 703 276 2889
Website: www.ncvc.org

Provides help for victims of crime in
the USA, either directly or through
state or federal partners, and training
for victim service providers. Also
works on education and policy issues.

Real Justice UK & Eire
PO Box 30, Todmorden OL14 6LA
Tel: 01706 810201
Fax: 01706 810793
E-mail: uk@realjustice.org
Website: www.realjustice.org

Provides training in restorative
conferencing.

Restorative Justice Consortium
c/o Society of Black Lawyers, Room 9,
Winchester House,11 Cranmer Road,
Kennington Park, London SW9 6EJ
Tel: 020 7735 6592
Fax: 020 7820 1389
E-mail:
national-office@sbl-hq.freeserve.co.uk
Website: www.restorative-justice.co.uk

Has a membership of national
organisations interested in promoting
restorative justice.

Thames Valley Police
Restorative Justice Consultancy, Police
Headquarters, Kidlington OX5 2NX
Tel: 01865 375218
Fax: 01865 375219
E-mail:
antony.walker@thamesvalley.police.uk

Provides training and consultancy in
restorative conferencing.

**Victim Offender Mediation
Association (VOMA)**
143 Canal Street, New Smyrna
Beach, FL 32168, USA
Tel: 001 904 424 1591
Fax: 001 904 424 6129
E-mail: voma@voma.org
Website: www.voma.org

Networking and information-sharing
in the field of victim/offender
mediation, mostly in the USA but
also elsewhere.

Victim Support National Office
Cranmer House, 39 Brixton Road,
London SW9 6DZ
Tel: 020 7735 9166
Fax: 020 7582 5712
E-mail: info@victimsupport.org.uk
Website: www.victimsupport.com

Network of local organisations that
provide support and practical help to
the victims of crime.

Youth Justice Board
11 Carteret Street, London
SW1H 9DL
Tel: 020 7271 3011
Fax: 020 7271 3020
E-mail: Helen.Powell@yjb.gsi.gov.uk
Website:
www.youth-justice-board.gov.uk

Provides development funding and
guidance to many restorative justice
(victim/offender mediation and
conferencing) projects involving
young offenders.

Index